The *Average* Buddhist Explores the Dharma

The Average Buddhist Explores the Dharma

Written by Barbara Wilson Arboleda
Illustrated by Teja Arboleda

Table of Contents

Introduction

Where I live, I usually feel uncomfortable when I'm asked about my religious preference. The word "Buddhist" kind of hangs in the air between me and whoever asks. The silence presses me for an explanation that's too complicated and too intimate to get into with a stranger who's had no exposure to the dharma. So, I usually just smile and nod.

Over time, the consistent feeling of being misunderstood led me to feel drawn toward connecting with other dharma-seekers. The subsequent growth of the Average Buddhist blog and online community has been immeasurably gratifying to develop. Through them, I have discovered an entire sangha of Buddhist practitioners of all backgrounds and philosophical orientations. Many are isolated from a community of people with whom they can discuss the dharma and its relevance to our culture, time and society.

The labels on the major sections of this book are a commentary on my experience working toward applying the dharma in my every day experience. I'm not a nun or a Rinpoche. I'm just an average American, small business owner, wife, mother, and community member. Some days I feel intimately connected to mindfulness. On other days, I'm not sure I even know what mindfulness is.

It is my hope that through the continued development of Average Buddhist we can encourage the growth of an American Buddhist experience that is both authentic and contributes to the well-being of all. Thank you for joining in conversation with me. I look forward to sharing your journey with you.

Section I: I Don't Get It

Precious Human Birth

I love watching my cats try to solve a problem. In many ways, their movements and expressions are not much different from my own or any other person I know. First, there's a moment of pause when the problem becomes evident, followed by a step back. Then comes the head cock to one side or the other. Finally one paw tentatively reaches out to try some solution or other. This same paw is likely to be quickly withdrawn when it becomes clear that the selected idea was unwise.

Even more human is their tendency to repeat the same solution several times before finally recognizing the need to reorient their approach. At this point, however, human and cat paths often diverge. Where a human would analyze the problem and attempt to mentally unravel its component parts, my cats would probably decide it was the right time to clean themselves.

The typical groovy New Age response to this observation would involve spouting adages about the cat's behavior being somehow more "natural", "genuine" or "better" and wouldn't the world be such a better place if we all just followed the cat's example. Truth be told, I'd rather not watch my neighbors on their porches cleaning themselves on a Sunday afternoon - or any other day - thanks any way.

Human society is more complicated than cat society and other people count on us to fulfill our roles in the community. To run off when the checkbook doesn't balance the first time would result in a cascade of cause and effect (karma) that could eventually be devastating for our families. The bath will simply have to wait.

Buddhism tells us though, it is only in this human form that we are able to achieve freedom from the cycle of birth and rebirth, known as samsara. Regardless of the number of lifetimes we have spent as cats, dogs or iguanas, it is only in this human lifetime that we have a chance to go all the way. It's a lot of pressure to put on less than a hundred years. Nonetheless, there it is.

So what can we do considering that we all need to feed the kids, wash the car and turn in that business report? If the entire human race dedicated itself to a monastic life, we'd have no progeny and our alms bowls would be empty. Let's face it. Working toward liberation needs to be a part-time pursuit for the Average Buddhist.

How can we do the work and live in the world? How can we remain engaged in our family and community and relinquish attachment at the same time? There is no one answer to this question that can be applied to us all. I offer these musings as a call to retain our sense of humor as we grapple with the enormity of the work that lies ahead.

If any of you find the universal solution, stand up and shout - Katz!

The Awakened One

One of my favorite lines from the movie *The Matrix* is the line where Morpheus tells Neo: "You have to understand, most of these people are not ready to be unplugged. And many of them are so inured, so hopelessly dependent on the system, that they will fight to protect it." The world proposed in *The Matrix* is not too far from what Buddhism proposes in that Buddhism urges us to understand that the things we perceive as tangible have no essential substance.

Despite its at times overwrought Neo-as-Christ analogy, *The Matrix* can also be interpreted in a Buddhist context to say that those who take the "red pill" awaken to an experience of the world they could not have imagined was possible. The word Buddha actually means "the awakened one". There's that one little hitch - in the movie our hero awakens to an utter dystopia, while Buddhism promises something much more fulfilling. Despite that promise, it is incredibly difficult to stay awake when our entire cultural enterprise is singing a constant mental lullaby.

Those who read the Average Buddhist blog may remember the post about the time I was craving a new cell phone cover. For some reason, my recent travels had taken me into the path of kiosks of the cutest darn phone covers ever! It's not that I didn't have the money. They weren't that expensive any way. Many years ago, I think I would have bought two or three covers without even thinking about it and swapped them out based on my mood. Ooh! I feel green today...no wait, Hello Kitty.

For whatever reason, I managed to muster up enough prajna to recognize that my current cell phone cover was in perfect condition and would only go to waste if I bought another one. Even more, I actually managed to ask myself what does it matter if my cell phone cover is cute? This was a true breakthrough for me.

Baby steps. Baby steps.

I was awake, but the craving was still there. Hmmm, maybe that thing about the dystopia is not so far off base after all. To be awake in the Buddhist sense of the word is to be present for all of the difficult emotions, thoughts and desires and to not run away from confronting them.

In the end, I did not buy a new cell phone cover, but one day in the coffee shop I took some of the stickers they use to cover the drinking spout on the take out cups and decorated the back of the cover I have.

Was that a compromise? Was I snoozing? Should I have stopped myself? Where is the line between intentional action and reflexive seeking of comfort? I know I smiled looking at the flowers when my phone was turned over...until they faded...and the sticky part started to smudge around...maybe the lesson was about impermanence all along.

"Why, oh why, didn't I take the blue pill!"

Ego-clinging

One of the most annoying experiences in my initiation to Buddhism was when I sat down with the JDPSN (Ji Do Poep Sa Nims - kind of like "honored teacher") at the Cambridge Zen Center for the first time and he asked me "Who are you?" Nothing I said was right. Here this guy doesn't know me from anyone else and he's presuming to tell me who I am? Rather, who I am not I should say because the dude never did give me an answer.

I started off with my name - nope. I told him what I did for work - nope. Then I decided he must be looking for the sort of crunchy-granola life-roles spiel. I am a daughter, a sister and a wife - no good. By this time I was getting a bit out of sorts and wanted to take that little stick out of his hand and say *You can't have this back until you're a good boy and tell me what I want to know. Now, who am I?* Even then, I had more self-control than that. So I chose to stare blankly at him. Unable to stare him down, I finally managed to squeak out *I don't know.*

Boom! Yes? What? That's right? Oh come on! *Stupid racka-fracka*...Hmmm...I never told him what I meant was "I don't know what the heck we're doing here." Shhhh...

As it turned out this lesson was one of those "slow burn" experiences that took some time to wrap my brain around. I started recognizing how easily I attached the words "I am" to different concepts. I am a singer. I am a singing teacher. I am a speech-language pathologist. I am a writer. I am an American. I am a Buddhist. It took quite some time for me to recognize the suffering that the application of these labels caused to me.

Having labels for all of these things I supposedly was caused me to identify with them to a level where I began to endlessly question and judge my own authenticity. If I'm a singer, but I'm not currently in a band, am I still really a singer? If I'm a singing teacher and I don't have all of the answers that my students need every day, am I really a singing teacher?

Conversely, the labels that I allowed others place on me became problematic as well. They say I am middle aged. So, now what? Does that change how I am supposed to feel? Do I have to suddenly stop dancing and start talking about my health problems to everyone who will listen? Do I have to start having health problems to fit the mold? It's all just senseless suffering. All I am is what is occurring at this moment. The next moment "I" and everything around me may have changed.

In 2010, I went to California to attend a voice course being led by one of my voice science mentors, Katherine Verdolini, in conjunction with her mentors, Arthur Lessac and Mark Madsen. They are all incredible people, but it is Mark's story that struck a chord with me in regard to ego-clinging.

Mark was already a successful and sought-after singing teacher in 2001, when he hit a deer while driving full speed on the highway. In this accident, he sustained a cervical spinal cord injury that left him quadriplegic. Since that time, he has been tirelessly working to have the fullest life and the fullest function possible. He has accomplished incredible feats of progress and found a way to continue his life's work.

When he told the story though, he included the fact that he had a really cool new car he was very proud of at that time. To hear him tell it, he appeared to be expressing some kind of identification with the car at that time. He said it never occurred to him the last time he walked to the car and sat in it that it would be the last time he would ever be able to use his legs.

In that accident, he lost the car, but he also lost things that most of us consider fundamental to our identity. He lost the ability to be: a person who walks, a person with complete independence, a person no one would look on with pity. Somehow he was able nonetheless to draw upon his inner essence to continue being with himself and with the world and to continue sharing his gifts.

Would I be able to let go of my own ego clinging to make such a remarkable transformation? I don't know.

Attachment

You know how it goes. You look in the closet and see the shirt you haven't worn in three years and say, I should just get rid of it. So, you pull it out of the closet and put it on your bed. Maybe you even get as far as taking it off the hanger, when suddenly you think, well...

Better yet, you look at the porcelain duck tureen you got for your wedding, that you've never used, and think, *This has really got to go.* So you go to the basement door and head down the stairs, but you stop and think, *but they'll be so hurt if they find out we didn't like it...*

Maybe instead it's the blue jeans that are missing all of their fabric from a six-inch region around each kneecap. The butt area below the left back pocket is almost see-through and you finally got out to the store to buy a new pair. You're heading toward the trashcan with the rumpled mess in a ball, when you suddenly think, *Awww, I had such great times in these jeans. I remember tailgating at that Jimmy Buffett concert...*

It happens to all of us. By the time we're adults most of us are surrounded by mounds of things, most of which we never even look at let alone use. Near where I live, there are a lot of old houses - built in late-1800's/early-1900's old. One thing that is striking about these houses is that no matter how large they are, there are very few closets. Where did people put things? Most likely, they didn't.

It's absurd how much stuff we have and how "sentimental" it is. We have become experts at inventing excuses for why we can't possibly get rid of this or that.

- *Fear*: What if I need it some day and can't afford it
- *Other people*: I don't want to hurt their feelings
- *Anthropomorphism*: My old Teddy bear looks so sad in the garbage bag
- *Clinging to the past*: I just need to know it's still there

Regardless of the excuse, holding onto things that are no longer useful to us is a burden. We need the space to store it. We need to dust it. When we move, we need to pack it up and haul it to another location. If we collect enough things, it crowds us in and leaves us cluttered with less physical and mental space to move around in. These attachments make us suffer in big ways and small.

My husband and I have had the dubious pleasure of holding onto other people's "stuff" during their life transitions; mostly because we have a basement. What's interesting is how quickly things accumulate and never go away – and it's not even our stuff. Someone was attached enough to these things that they wrapped and boxed them, taped them up and carried or shipped them to us to for safekeeping - then they never ask for it...ever.

Once, my husband tried asking one of these people if we could get rid of the things we'd been holding onto (for over a decade). An emphatic "no" was the response. He needed that stuff. Okaaaaay...

I've been practicing getting rid of a piece of clothing for every piece I buy for a while. This has at least ensured that all of my clothes (yes for all seasons) fit into one closet. Lately, I've been getting a little bolder. I've started looking at all of my things every week or two and trying to part with at least one item. So far, I've managed to find more than one thing I can dispense with each week. I'm sure it will get harder as I whittle away the chaff. I'll rub up against some of my more entrenched attachments, but I'm willing to see how far I can take it before I cry "Uncle."

At least the duck tureen made it out the door. It's a start.

No Ground

Mel Brooks said it in *History of the World: Part 1*, "It's good to be the king!" That's what we all really want - control. It is so fundamental to our current cultural orientation it is codified into one of the most referenced rubrics for the stages of a child's development, Erikson's Stages of Psychosocial Development. In Stages Two and Three, the child needs to develop personal control and control over the environment - all before age five. Failure to master this results in feelings of shame, guilt and doubt.

I guess that explains why most people are riddled with shame, guilt and doubt. It's not possible to exert complete control over oneself, let alone the environment. There are other factors involved; too much we can't anticipate. There is never a time we are totally in control - ever.

When we fail to control our world, as we inevitably do, we spend hours pouring through self-help books and attending workshops on how to seize the day in every situation. When we're done, we fail again. So we return.

The fact that we are capable of feeling in control of things for brief periods of time is one of the great punch lines of the universe on humanity. This illusion gives us hope that if we do things just right we can be Masters of the Universe! Um, no. Depending on your demeanor, you either think I am the biggest spoilsport ever, or you are relieved to be finally packing away your Xena cosplay suit.

That we're not in complete control of our lives is not our fault. There are some who would like us to believe that complete control lies just beyond the next dose of "5-Hour Energy". Kick up that adrenaline and I can make it through the hundred-mile bike ride. Uphill. All the way. In the rain. They confuse control with mania.

There are some who would have us believe complete control lies in compliance to generally accepted "shoulds" of society. Get a college degree. Get a job, save money, buy a house. Under this universal law, where is the possibility of lay off, sudden illness or economic recession?

There is nothing any of us can do to insulate ourselves from unpredictability. All we can do is act in our own best interest to increase the probability that things will turn out the way we'd like, but even a very high probability is no guarantee of success.

Some scientists argue there is no such thing as freewill; that the entire universe is predetermined by laws of cause and effect. I wouldn't go so far. Simple observation shows us turning on the oven will increase the *probability* that your pumpkin pie will bake. Sure, the vagaries of the universe may cause the pilot light to go out (unknown to you), leading you to spill the pie contents all over the floor an hour later before you realize it's still liquid...true story.

As one scientist told me, there's really only a high probability that the sun will rise each day. There is a high probability I will wake up in the morning; it's not a certainty. In the United States, even people of modest means can be relatively certain the lights will come on when they flip the switch, clean water will flow from the tap and their children will have shoes. In many other parts of the world, none of those things have a high probability.

Even those people who believe they are king, such as the despots toppled in the Arab Spring, lived under the illusion of complete control. They paid dearly for their illusion of control in karmic debt for the harm they have done. Despite their machinations probability still failed them and they were deposed.

Maybe it's not too late for Mel Brooks to change his phrase: It's *probably* good to be the king.

Impermanence

Have you ever seen those Buddhist monks who spend years constructing mandalas out of sand, grain by grain, only to wipe it away soon after it's finished? Me too. I'm sorry, but can you imagine? What's the point?

Okay, you're all good American Buddhists (or at least exploring this philosophy). You know the answer to this. Anyone? Bueller? Bueller?

I would like to stand up for impermanence. Sometimes, impermanence is a very good thing. It's a good thing that my hair grew out after I bleached it orange when I was 16. (Darn you, Nick Rhodes!) I'm glad the snow melts in the spring and it gets warm again. The fact that my teenager will not remain a puddle of hormones for the rest of her life is a blessing.

There are times, however, when impermanence hangs over us like the blade of a guillotine. We know things will change. We just don't know when.

- My grandmother just turned 93 years old.
- In about a year there will be major construction in the square where my business is located
- The bed and breakfast I'm writing in survived hurricane Irene
- We've capped the oil well in the Gulf of Mexico
- English is the lingua franca of the business world

Any of that could change in the next moment, never mind tomorrow.

One of my students told me that he and his significant other went to see an exhibit about Pompeii at the Boston Museum of Science. Talk about impermanence. Here are a bunch of people going about their business on a typical day and BOOM. It's inconceivable that an entire city could be buried in less than a day.

Fortunately, most of us will never be faced with utter annihilation. Still the daily experience of impermanence wears on everyone. The repeated loss of things and people we love makes us suffer. It's death by a thousand cuts.

I've recently been considering impermanence in terms of family photographs. Given that we are all now taking digital photos of our lives, the images are more ephemeral than ever. They exist as 1's and 0's on a hard drive somewhere and one electromagnetic event could wipe out these souvenirs of our family histories. When electronic formats change, we could find that old photographs passed down from previous generations are inaccessible to us. It could just be a darn shame that we've committed our family legacies to something as impermanent as the digital realm, but not necessarily.

Consider that in the age of physical photography, a house fire or tornado could irrevocably destroy the entire photographic record of your life. Now, if you use any kind of sharing or storage service like Flickr or Shutterfly, you will be able to retrieve your images in the event of a personal disaster and reprint anything you'd like to. Also, as eminently impermanent as digital pictures appear, they are so much more easily shared and distributed to the family and friends who are featured in them.

Think too about how many stranded family photographs end up in town center antique shops around the country. The names and faces are forever estranged. Haven't most of these images outlived their usefulness? I don't even want to consider the poor people who end up plastered on cheesy greeting cards with speech bubbles extolling the virtues of moonshine for your 50th birthday. Perhaps there is a place for impermanence even within a family history.

Maybe one day, they'll invent a camera which images self-destruct over the period of about 50 or 60 years. The timer would reset every time someone actually viewed it or printed it. The rest, like a mandala of sand would be released, loved and lost.

Shenpa

I am a professional shenpa magnet. This was something I didn't know until I listened to Pema Chödrön's *Getting Unstuck*. Until that time, I'd never heard of the word shenpa at all. Triggered. Hooked. Gotchya. Man, she has me pegged. Getting rid of shenpa? I don't know. You're on your own for that one.

The best I can figure is that working with dissolving shenpa is something like being a forensic detective. By the time you realize shenpa has kidnapped you, the crime has already been committed. You have to conduct a full investigation into the causes and circumstances of it. You need to collect fingerprints, talk to witnesses and then - just maybe - you can begin to develop some prajna about how the thief got away and where to find him.

Once I started thinking about it. I realized I have been dealing with mountains of shenpa my entire life. When Pema described the phenomenon as the preverbal experience of tightening that results from a perceived threat to your fundamental understanding of your "agreement" with the world, I immediately knew exactly what she was talking about.

Years before I became a Buddhist, I recognized this phenomenon. I just didn't have a word for it. I suffered from a mental pattern where I would feel agitated for no apparent reason. The feeling would appear suddenly in a variety of benign situations, manifesting as a general sense of squirming unease, perhaps overlaid with anger or anxiety. Even then, I started a practice of noticing when this feeling arose, pausing immediately and rewinding the previous few minutes' events until I found the trigger. What I discovered was fascinating.

I learned it took very little to get my shenpa mousetrap to spring. Maybe I heard something I didn't like of the news. Maybe I briefly recalled a confrontational conversation with a colleague the day before. Maybe I had just read an annoying letter from a government agency. Maybe I remembered something unpleasant I had to do that day. What surprised me was how mundane most of the triggers were.

Fortunately, I also discovered that mundane triggers of shenpa are easy to dissolve. Usually, once I touched on the root causes of these small agitations and examined their relevance to my feelings, I was able to release myself from the hooks that made them stick with me. Major triggers, not so much.

For larger shenpa events, it is relatively easy to determine what the essential problem is: e.g., I think she hates me. Where my internal police work fails me is in determining a motive and suspect in the crime. Why do you think that she hates you just because she hasn't answered your email from three days ago? I can often observe what is happening, but I can't perceive why. Like a rash of robberies, I can't make it stop until I know who or what to arrest.

I wonder sometimes if there's some kind of shenpa self-defense course I can take. Maybe I could work up a few good kung fu moves to toss it off when it tries to accost me again. I could try S-I-N-G like Sandra Bullock in Miss Congeniality: solar plexus, instep, nose, groin! Now where exactly is the solar plexus of an emotion? Ouch! Oops. Missed.

If you find it, let me know.

Craving

Have you ever walked into a store and wanted to buy something; it didn't matter what, just something? Weird, huh? For me, that happens at Staples all the time. There's a Staples a few blocks away from my office. Sometimes only the perils of crossing Route 1, the small highway that divides the store from the center of town, keeps me from succumbing to its siren song.

I must admit I've always loved office supplies. When I was in college, I worked at the campus bookstore between classes. One day, the sad state of the school/office supplies area finally got to me. I asked the manager if I could do a redesign of that area. From then on, I was hooked. Before long, I was managing the department, meeting with vendors from Faber Castell and Avery. Learning about all the new exciting developments in pen technology. The gel pen was new back then. Ahhhhh.

So, here I am more than two decades later and I'm still drawn to the neat pegs of highlighters and pencils and shelves of multicolored Post It notes and tab dividers. Walking into Staples has developed its own sense memory for me as powerful as the memory of walking into Grossman's with my dad when I was a kid. Just being there makes me feel like I need something.

This is the true power of craving. Most of the time it's so darn diffuse, manifesting as a mild ache for something we can't define. There is only the uncomfortable feeling that something is missing. If something is missing then we should be able to lay down a few bucks and fix that up soon enough, right? Man, I wish.

In the same period of time I was starting my foray into the world of office supplies mogul at the school bookstore, I was studying Maslow's Hierarchy of Needs in class.

Abraham Maslow was an American psychologist who was one of the first to intensely study the psychology of people who were not considered mentally ill. He created a little pyramid-shaped diagram that was designed to describe the order in which "normal" people have their needs fulfilled.

At the bottom of Maslow's pyramid are physiological needs such as food, water and sleep. Once these needs are fulfilled, a person can be progress to the next layer of needs. In his theory this would be safety needs such as health, employment and property. There are five steps to the top, which is called self-actualization.

Included in self-actualization are needs such as spontaneity, creativity and social justice. The fact that self-actualization rests at the top of the pyramid indicates it is the highest level of human achievement. The fact that the pyramid shape makes self-actualization the smallest area of the pyramid indicates that the fewest number of people are able to achieve that level of development. I argue no one does.

A recent report in Time Magazine stated that money does actually buy happiness - until you are making $75,000 a year. Beyond that, money does not improve a person's overall feeling of wellbeing or satisfaction with life. Still most people crave making much more than that. The punch line of Maslow's hierarchy of needs is the fact that the unenlightened human being is not capable of being self-actualized. Once we achieve a goal, there is always something else to strive for. In this sense, Maslow's hierarchy of needs is in itself a set up for incessant craving.

By presenting self-actualization as a developmental objective that can be met and illustrating it in a finite space, we are fed the idea that not feeling self-actualized means we are somehow incomplete. Naturally then, there is something we have to go out and get or something we have to go out and do to finish our process of self-actualization. We're grasping at shadows.

Even the coolest multicolored gel pen won't help me express myself, if I have nothing to say. There is no folder into which I can stash the ideas of all the things I would like to accomplish in my lifetime. Maybe I should go out some night and disable the crosswalk lights for Route 1.

Suffering

The first Noble Truth: life is suffering. Cool! Sign me up! Sounds great! I can't wait! Hold on. We can overcome it? Whew. I was worried there for a second. And worrying is suffering, which means I haven't overcome it, which means...!!!!!

Shortly after September 11, 2001 our national security apparatus invented the color-coded Threat Advisory Scale. Intended as a concrete way to conceptualize the current risk of terrorist attack, the scale quickly became a regular feature in news programs, especially in stories about travel. The highest level of danger was red. Increased safety followed the colors on the way down through orange, yellow, blue and green. The color-coded scale was discontinued in 2011. According to Wikipedia at the time of this writing, it never was lowered to blue or green - ever.

My brother and I joked around about it one day. At the time, the government frequently told all Americans to be in a "heightened state of alert". My brother is a pretty low-key guy, who works in finance. Like me though, he has a hyperbolic sense of humor. He said, "I don't know what I should be doing to be in a heightened state of alert. I mean, should I run out in the middle of the street waving my arms around shouting "I'm in a heightened state of alert! Ahhhhhh!'" He had a point. We were already taking off our shoes before getting on a plane. What more were we supposed to do?

Meanwhile, in London, there were successful bomb attacks. I traveled to London between the two sets of subway bombings in July 2005 and was in the city during the second attack. I have to say; those Brits were really collected and organized about the whole thing. Sure, throughout my trip there were messages on TV telling people to be vigilant, but there was a practicality to it that was missing from my experience of the color-coded Threat Scale at home. In Britain, they told you to be vigilant and then told you what to be vigilant about. Not rocket science, but effective.

The system worked well enough, in fact, that I experienced several train evacuations over dropped pencils or forgotten shopping bags. Who can blame them when they were only a week out from an actual event? Surprisingly, even the evacuations were orderly and everyone (that I encountered) was patient about it.

These two stories provide contrasting responses to suffering that are relevant to understanding its insidious nature. On the one hand, is a population of people who are simply told to worry. On the other hand is a population that is given practical advice for concrete things they can do. Who suffers more? I argue that American society suffered enormously under this system and by the fact that we never achieved a color-coded announcement of general safety.

The insight into suffering in general is the truth that much of our suffering occurs in response to things that lack substance or positive response. We suffer when we worry about what awaits us in the future and suffer more when we are led to believe that there is nothing we can do to guide that future. We suffer when we regret the past and suffer more when we are led to believe that we could have done more to prevent bad things from happening. This is what tears us apart more than any event ever could.

So until I have better guidance in terms of how to contribute to the general safety of my community, the only waving around I'll doing with my arms while yelling will be at a Duran Duran concert. Woo hoo! Hey, they're from England too. Maybe they have some advice to share.

Emptiness

Quantum physics has scientifically defined what the historical Buddha discerned intuitively over two thousand years ago. Nothing we perceive is solid. Every object we see is merely a marker location for an increased density of clustering atoms. There continue to be atoms between each "object" and every other, in essence connecting them, but there appears to be separation because the density of the atoms is so much lower in the "in between" than among the atoms that are participating in the group activity we might see as "chair-ing" (being a chair) or "coffee-ing" (being coffee).

That the universe is largely comprised of space at both a macro and a micro level has now entered the lexicon of the average American through the popular media. Movies such as Inception play with these concepts as well. Still it's difficult to conceive of. The smallest atom we know of is the hydrogen atom with its proton and single electron. This atom is more than 99% empty space. If you are interested in seeing a graphical representation of this, I found a nice one here:

http://www.phrenopolis.com/perspective/atom

Scrolling all the way to the right provides a glimpse into the massive scale of this truth.

If the computer keyboard I am typing on is mostly empty space, then how can my thoughts and feelings have any essential substance? Atoms in their coziness with other atoms - as a coffee cup, let's say - create an electromagnetic field that other atoms - my hand, let's say - skate across. A thought creates an electric impulse that is transmitted across brain cells. Neither is solid. All things are predicated on this balance of positive and negative electric elements that both binds and repels.

That our five senses are incapable of discerning the spaces between things speaks to their limitations as agents of observation. Moving beyond physical perception is indeed a feat of great measure, but this is what Buddhist practice is all about. As Buddhists we are engaged in grand experimentation with our minds to figure out how to see things as they really are.

I didn't understand any of this when I was first drawn to Buddhism. Discussions of emptiness had no resonance for me. In my ego-clinging I was so strongly identified with the observations of my five senses that I was convinced of the essential reality of both things and thoughts. Energy didn't play into it at the time. To be honest, I am still strongly identified with the observations of my five senses. The progress I have made has been largely in my ability to question what I perceive.

There was one dharma talk I attended where the teacher described the process of Buddhist contemplation like this: First, you look at a mountain and a mountain is a mountain. When you begin practicing Buddhism, a mountain is a pencil, a mountain is a ball of clay, a mountain is a puff of air. Finally, when you have been practicing for many years you begin to understand. A mountain is a mountain. I think my mountain is still a pencil, but at least there are things I can do with that.

Section II: I Think I Get It

"Don't Know" Mind

There is immense pressure for us all to make firm decisions. In every sphere, we are consistently challenged to take a stand and stick to it. Think about the way in which young people are bothered at an early age with the question *What do you want to be when you grow up?* I can't help but think to myself, She's six. What do you think she wants to be? A ballerina, a singer and an actress.

In our practical, get-right-to-it culture, we are given very little room in which to admit we don't know. After a cursory analysis of the facts of any given situation, we are supposed to make up our minds. Political campaigns have been degraded to sound bites. Our doctors are supposed be able to whip off a diagnosis and prescription with barely a health history. Even higher education has been stripped of much of the training in critical thinking and exploration of topics of curious interest. Instead, every course is expected to pull its weight in terms of practicality, which is to say that it has to directly apply to what we have decided we are going to do for a profession.

I was raised Episcopalian. It is not a particularly oppressive denomination, but the liturgy still revolves around the Nicene Creed (a.k.a. the Apostle's Creed), which is a statement of belief in the fundamental tenets of Christianity. In it are statements about the conceptualization of God, the Virgin birth and the spiritual identity of Jesus as Son and Savior. In this worldview, there is no "don't know".

It was during a Sunday service in 1992 when I realized, somewhat abruptly, I could not remain a Christian. I was reciting the Nicene Creed like I had hundreds of times before as an altar girl and later as a congregant. Suddenly I knew I didn't believe many of the things I was saying. At that time, I didn't know what it was that I did believe. Yet my mouth was speaking words of certainty that weren't true to me.

This crisis of faith prompted a quest to learn about as many religions as I could. I can't say that my investigation was particularly scientific. I let inspiration draw me to various quarters and gave my mind the freedom to connect the dots as it saw fit. There were plenty of people I met who had given up all together, deciding to construct their own religions. Something told me though that in the entire collection of human wisdom about the divine and the nature of the universe, there must be other people who thought the way I did. I was determined to find them.

As a part of this project, I conducted interviews with people of a variety of religious backgrounds. I thought at the time that I might turn them into some kind of article, but that never materialized. Nonetheless, I was fascinated by the myriad ways in which people grapple with the mysteries of life. I interviewed a Christian Scientist, a conservative Jewish rabbi, an excommunicated Mormon, a Methodist priest, and one of the spiritual-not-religious, among others. In general, the amount of certainty the interviewees expressed was high. I wasn't sure of anything. Furthermore, I didn't think I was supposed to believe I understood it all. In this philosophy, for quite some time I found myself alone.

It was the *Tibetan Book of Living and Dying* by Sogyul Rinpoche that introduced me to Buddhism and through which I found my spiritual home. Reading that book, I knew I was finally on the right track even though I didn't feel I'd found the right form. It wasn't until several years later, through Kwan Um Zen that I was introduced to the vocabulary of "don't know mind" and my inner singing bowl started ringing. Over ten years later, I still don't understand the true nature of the universe, the world or myself. In "don't know mind" I can take refuge in the knowledge that that is as it should be - for now.

What is the nature of "god"? I don't know. What is the nature of the chair I am sitting on? I don't know. What do I want to be when I grow up? Well, duh! A ballerina, a singer, an actor. Beyond that, I don't know.

Karma

It's funny the way Americans have distorted the concept of karma. With our trademark cynicism, one popular understanding is that karma is some kind of system of retribution for wrongdoing. *Man, that guy who just cut me off is gonna have some bad karma coming his way!*

Conversely, for some it is perceived a kind of Frequent Flier Program where you can save up good karma points against future sin. My understanding of karma swung between those interpretations for many years, guided more by the convenience of the situation than by any real thought of karma as true force of nature.

In that vein, my husband and I used to jokingly refer to one of our friends as a "karma sucker". He was always doing favors for us and helping out with things. Frequently, he cooks us multi-course extravaganza dinners with fancy ingredients like Emerald Frizz and broccoli rabe. After a while I started to wonder if there was some shadowy cosmic debt we were accumulating. *Quick! Find someone to help! I've got to build up my karma again before S. comes over!*

A simplistic understanding of karma is inevitable, given the framework within which most Western practitioners were raised. There is sin and repentance, crime and punishment, regret and confession. The Western notion of consequence is linear and direct. If you do this bad thing, this other bad thing will happen to you. The Buddhist idea of karma is not so dualistic.

Karma in the Eastern sense is more like Schrodinger's Cat Box. There is a set of circumstances from which a number of possible future circumstances may arise, simultaneously or at an undetermined point in the future. There is always room for the cat to act in ways that may or may not impact the shifting of its future circumstances.

Note that I say "circumstances" and not "consequences". While certainly there is a large element of cause and effect present in the workings of karma, the effects of our actions are not inherently good or bad. Instead, our circumstances provide us with an opportunity to continue to grow and develop spiritually.

In the West, there is also a problem of attribution. Have you ever noticed we have a tendency to assume that people in bad circumstances must have brought them on themselves? *Better start pulling your weight, buddy!* Conversely, when we find ourselves in bad circumstances it is usually attributed to the influence of some outside force. When we are in good circumstances though, we tend to attribute it to our own meritorious actions. *Yeah, me!*

What if...you are presented with people in unfortunate circumstances because it's you who needs to learn to be more giving? What if...you are in fortunate circumstances because your mother's merits earned *her* the comfort of knowing her child is doing well? You just don't know, do you?

So...better start pulling your weight, buddy!

I mean, our karmic history is not something we generally have access to. Perhaps we're not supposed to. Knowing precisely when and if we have been meritorious and the extent to which we have failed to engage in right thought and right action has enormous potential to either make us pompous or paralyzed in fear of making things worse. Best to maintain your focus on the now in deciding how to behave, because you can't dupe the system.

As far as S. is concerned, I'll just let him take the merit. Hopefully that means I have some to spare. In the meantime, I'll drown my doubt in a serving of broccoli rabe.

The Middle Way

Have you ever looked at one of those images of a paunchy Buddha and asked yourself How does a travelling ascetic who meditates all day get a belly like that? Okay, it's irreverent, but I have wondered on occasion.

My first image of Buddha came from two statues my grandmother had in her house. One of them is now on my personal altar. Grandma was not a Buddhist, but she had the fascination with all things "oriental" that many from her generation shared. She had oriental rugs and black lacquer furniture, satin drapes and a Japanese style painting of a mountain in the stairwell to the basement family room. Her entire house smelled vaguely of incense, even though I never saw her burning any.

My grandmother told me it was good luck to rub Buddha's belly. In fact, what she thought was a universal practice was limited to images of Budai, who was not the historical Buddha but monk in the 10th century CE. As for most Westerners, however, for my grandmother a Buddha, was a Buddha, was a Buddha.

With increased exposure to images of Buddha, I have now seen many sizes and shapes of Buddha's belly. On the portliness scale, the Buddha I got from Grandma is somewhere in the middle. She never realized how appropriate this is given the historical Buddha's conclusions about the Middle Way. Of course, he didn't start out so moderately.

The first time reading the beginning of the spiritual path of Siddhartha Gautama, I thought *What a jerk!* After all, he abandoned his wife, son and position to go a-wanderin' and "find himself". How many times has that scene been played out in human history? As an aside, I would love to know how he came to have his son as a follower. I'm sure it's somewhere in some book I haven't read yet. But that's neither here nor there.

What is important to consider from our modern perspective is that Buddha discovered a harsh, ascetic life did not produce the results he was looking for. Total denial of what this world had to offer did not bring him closer to enlightenment. Instead, he found there is a "middle way", neither ascetic nor hedonistic, that allows us to develop discipline while providing enough friction with life to help us move forward.

Whew! What a relief. I mean, I want enlightenment as much as the next person, but asceticism? Given where I'm approaching the practice from, I'd end up reincarnated as a hamster.

So after further consideration, Siddhartha Gautama's life is inspiring for the Buddhist laity. In itself it justifies the fact that the Buddhist laity has just as much opportunity as any monk or nun to find the truth, even if you have a little belly to show for your life.

Mindfulness

Many years ago, I worked at a mortgage company in a data entry position. It was a typical cube farm in a typical office with typical water cooler conversations throughout the day. One day, a colleague enthusiastically told us about her newborn niece. She told us how alert the baby was and how smart. After all, if you put her in front of the television, she could watch it for hours. (Okay, not hours. I exaggerate because I don't remember exactly what she said, but it was a really long time for a baby.) I felt like the only one who caught this non sequitur, since everyone else was nodding and smiling. It seems our training in distraction begins at a young age.

Since then, the distractions we present to young children have grown in intrusiveness and in sophistication. Television is no longer the sole source of senseless light and movement. Every toy is constructed from multiple, color-clashing plastics. Every toy makes noise. Too many are associated with a large corporate media branded personality. And we wonder why Attention Deficit Hyperactivity Disorder is so rampant.

When I studied neurology in graduate school, I learned that there are different levels of attention, arranged roughly hierarchically in terms of the cognitive load it places on the brain. These were focused attention, sustained attention, alternating attention and divided attention. Since then, neuroscientists have pretty much debunked divided attention all together. It seems that what we perceive to be divided attention is in fact rapidly alternating attention, which does impact the quality of the attention that is allocated to each task. In our fast-paced "multitasking" world, this is terribly inconvenient. Instead of being disappointed though, I suggest we see it as a call to revive the lost art of day-to-day mindfulness.

As a business owner, I am pulled in many directions at once. I have to see clients while maintaining all of the practical elements of keeping things running smoothly. It is too easy to get caught up in the fervor of trying to get everything done at once. Time and again, I convince myself that I can simultaneously work on three tasks at the same time. Inevitably I get tangled up in my thoughts and everything comes to a grinding halt. It all ends with me staring at my computer screen thinking...well, thinking everything at once and nothing at all.

The times that I manage to reign myself in and maintain a focus on just one thing, to give it all of my attention and maintain awareness of each action I am taking to complete the task, the more easily and efficiently I am able to get it done. If I am to be truly honest with myself, it usually takes less time than it would have if I had mentally checked out of the process.

What's more important, mindfulness seems to put me in "the zone" for whatever I am working on. It centers my mind similarly to meditation, reducing the stress of whatever task is before me. Since stress is suffering, mindfulness simply feels better.

Sometimes I wonder what happened to the little baby I learned about in 1991. She'd be in college by now. Maybe her aunt was right. Maybe she has a remarkable ability to focus and she is constructing treatises that will lead to the end of world hunger. Or. Maybe she's cutting and pasting into a Google Doc from Wikipedia while her nails are drying and replaying the same "cute kitten" video on YouTube until her eyes water. It's hard to know. I hope it's the former.

Meditation

In his book *The Accidental Buddhist*, Dinty Moore refers to his inability to focus during meditation as "monkey mind". I can relate to that. I can be walking to work, enjoying the day, practicing noticing all of the sounds I can detect - one of my favorite walking meditations - when suddenly I think about how mad I am at that jerk who ignored me and who I had to chase in a thousand phone calls to get the answer to a simple question...or something similar.

The dialogue in my mind sounds a lot like that scene in the movie *The Incredibles*, where the bad guy, Syndrome, has Mr. Incredible tied up and instead of killing him, Syndrome starts going on about how wonderful he is. *I am Syndrome!* Finally, he realizes this and says, *Oh ho ho! You sly dog. You got me monologuing. I can't believe it!* My mind is kind of like that. It's never still.

Scratch that, it was still. Once. For about three seconds. It happened at some Zen center I don't remember the name of. In the middle of the meditation, the leader instructed us to turn around and face the other direction, which put me face-to-face with a blank white wall. Ping! A moment of absolutely nothing. Of course, the elation that followed ruined the whole thing. I got it right! Oh, darn. Shenpa.

At least I know I'm not alone. Pema Chödrön admits to having a "terribly discursive mind and this awful meditation" that doesn't bother her any more. If Pema doesn't meditate "right", I guess I can cut myself some slack. After all, she's been at it much longer than I have and in much more ideal circumstances.

It's funny to me that mediation instruction - even for beginners - revolves around sitting and staying still. I usually come closest to a meditative state when I'm moving. Dancing truly clears my head. Walking usually brings me closer to center, especially walking through a graveyard. Bowing and yoga sweeps the dust out of certain corners of my mind. Get me seated though and it's pretty much all over. If I don't fall asleep, I fidget. If I don't fidget, I think. If I think, I get hooked. If I get hooked, I start monologuing.

I am Syndrome, your nemesis and...come back to the breath...

I am Syndrome!

<sigh>

This is usually about the time the inferiority complex kicks in. Everyone says you have to do sitting meditation as a part of the practice. If I can't do sitting meditation, I can't really be a Buddhist. Oh yes, I can hear all the Bodhisattva's laughing now. There's nothing like attaching yourself to labels and using the teachings against yourself to make you feel like a true American Buddhist.

It seems to me that sitting meditation is actually something of an advanced practice for those who live in a society of hyper-doing. Perhaps one of the reasons that mediation feels inaccessible to most Americans is that going from moving a mile a minute to zero is to big a leap to make all at one time. The waves of a lake can't still themselves immediately after a pack of jet skiers rides by. Perhaps more people would feel successful and continue to develop the practice if we were to break the process down into progressively more still activities.

In the end, I believe what's important is to remain focused on the purpose, not the form of meditation. What do we meditate for? To impress each other with our iron man stamina? I hope not. The purpose of meditation is to develop our ability to experience our true nature and the true nature of the world around us. In the service of that, whatever works, dude.

At this time, Syndrome is an ever-present part of my mind space. He gets me monologing again and again. *Oh ho ho! You sly dog!* I trust that the more I practice stilling him, the more used to stillness my mind will become. The more used to stillness my mind is, I'm convinced the sitting will come.

Compassion

I work with people who have neurological disorders many of whom have dysarthria, a disorder that slurs articulation and makes normal speed impossible. The general population is not aware that dysarthria exists, or if they are it is not the first thing that comes to mind when a speech-disordered person approaches them. It doesn't help that many of the neurological issues impacting speech also disrupt facial symmetry, physical balance and walking pattern.

Early in my career, I learned to train my patients to introduce themselves this way: *Hello, I'm So-and-so. I have a problem with my speech. Please let me know if you have trouble understanding anything I say.* I came to this conclusion after hearing horror stories of my patients being cut off at bars, hung up on by people on the telephone and yelled at by counter clerks to "Go sober up!"

Coming right out and saying that they have a speech problem does the trick though. Once people are given a medical reason why my patients don't sound normal, they are usually as nice as can be. They offer extra support, extra time and extra attention. So, why is it that when the blanks are empty in terms of a reason why my patients' speech is slurred that people always fill the blank with something negative?

Think about your average daily experience. How many people do you really see stumbling around town blind drunk or whacked out on drugs? Yes, there are certain areas of the country where this is more likely than others, but by and large there are usually other clues to indicate that someone is drunk or high: slovenly appearance, smell of urine, alcohol on the breath, etc. The neurological patients I have worked with generally do everything they can to look (and smell) presentable.

On the other hand, think about this. In the United States, someone has a stroke every 40 seconds. One out of four strokes occur in people under age 65. Almost 800,000 people each year have a stroke in the United States. *http://www.strokecenter.org/patients/stats.htm (retrieved 10/10/2011)*

Many of these individuals will end up with dysarthria. Then consider all of the other disorders that cause dysarthria: Multiple Sclerosis, Parkinson's Disease, Bell's Palsy, Amyotrophic Lateral Sclerosis, ataxia, traumatic brain injury (think soldiers and car accidents, for example). The list goes on and on.

What this means is that there are a heck of a lot more people walking around the community with legitimate, neurologically based slurring of speech than there are drunks and drug addicts. So I ask again, why do most people default to thinking that someone is drunk or on drugs when they hear disordered speech?

I am convinced most people don't mean to lack compassion. When they are given the proper information many go out of their way to help, but there seems to be a true lack of mindfulness in terms of the expectation that there will be a need to be compassionate. I suggest that in Buddhist practice we should flip this habit around and apply compassion first. Beyond that, even when we are presented with someone who is drunk or on drugs, we must be on guard against our tendency to abandon compassion for disgust.

I'm sure there will be many people in your respective communities who won't understand this approach. May I suggest the following: *Hello, my name is Barbara. I'm a Buddhist. Please let me know if you have trouble understanding my desire to assist all sentient beings.*

Lovingkindness

Do unto others as you would have them do unto you. It's the Golden Rule. In the United States, we usually associate this with Christianity and an edict of Jesus, but many religions have versions of this same concept. It is a simple human recipe for the application of lovingkindness. What it doesn't take into account, however, is the fact that "as you would have them do unto you" can be very different for different people.

One morning, when I was home from college, my sister was in high school and my dad was away on business, I heard my mom yelling from downstairs. "Amy! Mouse! There's a mouse! Amy!" My sister is the animal person in the family. So, naturally she was the go-to person for any mouse "situation." Neither my sister nor I wake up easily in the morning. I continued with my face stuffed in the pillow while I heard my sister stumble out of her room.

"Amy!"

My sister announced she was coming and shuffled down the stairs.

After that, I couldn't make out their words, but clearly my sister was taking charge and my mother was still upset. There was a brief swell in the activity and my mother shouted, "I don't care. Get rid of it!" This was followed by more mumble, mumble. Finally, my sister lurched back upstairs to her room and closed the door again.

Here's the story as I got it after the fact. My mother, an early riser, woke up and went downstairs to make some coffee. She walked back and forth in the kitchen a few times before she noticed a "dead mouse" lying in front of the kitchen sink. This is when the commotion started.

When my sister came downstairs, she assessed the situation and promptly announced, "Mom, it's not a mouse. It's a vole." This prompted the "I don't care" exchange. My sister figured out that our cats had caught the unfortunate vole, killed it and placed it deliberately where they knew my mother spent time to give her a gift.

Apparently, cats believe we humans are inconceivably inept hunters. After all, there's no chasing and slaughtering going on in most households and all the cats get are various textures of brown mealy material. In the cats' minds, we could use some help. So, when given the opportunity, they do unto others as they would have done unto themselves.

So, my sister told my mother that she had hurt the cats' feelings because they were only doing what they thought was something good to support the pack and got negative consequences for it. You can imagine how that went over.

As people we frequently deposit voles on the floor by each other's kitchen sinks, usually without even realizing it. We make jokes about it in comedy sketches where someone insists on helping an elderly person to the other side of a street they didn't want to cross in the first place. How many times must I tell people who don't know my house *not* to help me clean up the kitchen after dinner? I have a way I like things and places where things belong. If someone who doesn't know my routine "helps" me, it only makes more work for me later on.

There is an aspect to lovingkindness that is much more complicated than the Golden Rule would imply. In order to really accomplish the goal, you need to pay attention to what makes the other person feel good, regardless of what you want. If they actually want a vole at their kitchen sink in the morning, great! Otherwise, you'll have to be a little more creative than that.

Nirvana

It took me a while to realize that my understanding of nirvana was completely skewed. Popular culture has somewhat absconded with the concept of nirvana and transformed it into something very unlike its "true nature". Nirvana in the United States is an unholy blend between being a synonym for heaven and being an experience you can buy.

What does the Average American picture when they think about nirvana? That depends upon their proclivities for personal relaxation. One might imagine lying in a bubble bath with incense and candles in the room, reading a good book. Someone else might see themselves skydiving on a clear day with their best friend. Then there are those who prefer being presented with a banquet of their favorite food laid out on fine china with crystal goblets for the wine. And for almost everyone, there's chocolate!

I suppose these images are at least partial truths. To the right person, any of the luxuries above would put them in a state where suffering has ceased. The problem for the Average Buddhist is that the ending of suffering brought about by each of these things is temporary. This is where the cultural understanding of nirvana and the dharma version of nirvana diverge.

Quite frankly, I'm still trying to wrap my brain around it all. I was surprised, when I read the first Average Buddhist book club selection, *One Dharma* by Joseph Goldstein, to learn how much disagreement there is among learned Buddhists regarding the nature of Nirvana. That it entails an end to suffering and an end to samsara (the cycle of birth and rebirth) seems to be a point of agreement. Then it all gets a little fuzzy.

Is nirvana more correctly experienced as a state of mind or as a place? For one who is enlightened but living, it appears there is an end to suffering and craving and that all thoughts and actions are karmically neutral. If you're still alive though, are you simultaneously "in" nirvana?

What really gets my eyes spinning though is the question of what happens to consciousness when nirvana is achieved. Some say that a luminous consciousness remains individuated enough that one can choose to return as a Bodhisattva. Others believe in the utter annihilation of self and the complete loss of differentiated consciousness. Some say that the state of nirvana is permanent. Others speak of it as just another bardo from which a being may be tossed out, if the cycle of samsara is activated again. Oops! I tripped...sorry...

If Buddhist monks and scholars can't agree on the nature of nirvana, how am I supposed to begin to conceptualize it? Do I want to go there? If I want to go there, then I have desire. If I have desire, the cycle of samsara is still turning. So, I can't go there. If I don't want to go there, then I can actually get there because I have no desire. The problem is I don't care any more. What if nirvana isn't really a place? Then what happens to the consciousness when we die? If I care, I'm stuck with samsara. Therefore, the point is moot. Oh my head!

No wonder people satisfy themselves with the simplification. Get me that chocolate...and a bubble bath!

Sangha

There are still relatively few Buddhists in the United States. This makes participating in a physical Buddhist sangha challenging. If you live in a major metropolitan area, there might be Zen center, a Shambhala center and some random meditation groups on college campuses, but they will be spread around. Usually they will be hard to get to by car and take hours to get to by public transportation. So, only those who live in the direct surrounding area will be able to get there with any regularity.

For the rest of us, the ability to be honest about our spiritual orientation remains a challenge. This is particularly true for those who live in areas where a large portion of the population lumps Buddhism in with atheism, paganism and other "devilish heathen" religions.

Technology has contributed much in terms of allowing like-minded individuals to create communities. I get immense joy from and feel fond friendship for the people I interact with on the Average Buddhist blog and in the Facebook and Google+ communities. Many people in these groups have expressed feelings like mine, that there is no feasible way to incorporate regular meetings with a Buddhist community into their lives where they live. For some, this has led to feelings of isolation and sadness.

Despite the fact that none of us have personally met, the technology gives us the opportunity to share ideas and questions about the dharma using language and concepts that others in our community would not understand. Virtual sanghas perform a vital service in terms of creating connectedness within a diasporic religious minority.

As wonderful as our online sangha is, we all know that our interactions in RL (real life) sustain us in a different way that is fundamental to our being. To address this reality, I have decided to expand my definition of sangha. Because any group of people (indeed, even one person) provides me with the opportunity for practice, I have chosen to include all of my social groups under the umbrella of "sangha". This includes my friends and family, colleagues, random people in cars, people I dislike, and all of the circles of people into which I come into contact. Buddhist/not-Buddhist. It doesn't matter. Perhaps this is what sangha is supposed to mean.

In folding these disparate people into my sangha, I have to translate my perspective so others who have no background in Buddhism can understand. Equally, I am learning to hear their perspectives in a new way. When they are speaking in terms of their own religious reality, if I listen carefully I can often map a core concept to a Buddhist principle. Where there is unkindness or hurtfulness, it can be mapped back to wrong words and wrong action.

At first, it may seem like I am devaluing others' spirituality by morphing their perspectives into Buddhism. I prefer to think of it as a mindful response to the inevitability of the need for code switching in life. Since we all see the world through our own value lens, it is up to each of us to bring our assumptions to a conscious level so we can evaluate our reaction to others before we act uncompassionately due to some semantic misunderstanding.

By spreading the blanket of sangha wide, we free ourselves from suffering alone-ness on the spiritual path. Though there may not be many Buddhists where you live, there are certainly sincere people whose faith includes translatable concepts such as compassion, mindfulness, right thought and right action. If we include them in our sangha, we will take time to translate concepts and care enough to share ourselves with the community in a way it can understand.

Section III: But I Don't Get It

Samsara

For most Americans, entering the world of Buddhist practice entails navigating a slew of foreign words describing concepts that are difficult to translate precisely. Samsara should not be one of these. You see, we have a perfectly good and beloved saying to communicate the concept of "samsara" - "Same shit, different day".

At first, I thought samsara referred simply to suffering itself. It wasn't until I dug into the teachings a little further that I understood it to be the cycle of birth and rebirth, the driving force behind suffering. Fortunately, it was then a short leap to understanding the cycle of birth and rebirth does not simply refer to physical birth and death, but also all of the shorter cycles that occur within our lives.

A friend of mine consistently dated jerks in high school and eventually married a man who treated her poorly. She experienced the birth and rebirth of the suffering borne by that behavior. Now that she has just remarried someone who treats her with the respect she deserves, that strand of suffering has come to an end.

I recently read *The Universe In A Single Atom* by the Dalai Lama. In Chapter 4, "The Big Bang and the Buddhist Beginningless Universe", he discusses the Buddhist principle of dependent origination, which itself springs from the dual truths of "impermanence" and "potentiality". He makes a point to separate physical dependent origination from the intentionality in consciousness that initiates karma. This closely correlates to my experience with and observations of the world around me. Sometimes, suffering happens because of a past disservice to sentient beings (in this lifetime or another). At other times, shit just happens.

So, here we all are manifest in physical form, even if we can manage to cleanse our intentions and live in service to the benefit of sentient beings, we can still be swept away along with 200,000 other people by a tidal wave arising from unconscious dependent origination that may have been initiated a million years ago.

Unfortunately for us, we are rarely able to discern whether the events and patterns we experience in our lifetime are the result of karmic forces or physical dependent origination. Even if we could, I'm not sure it would help us cope with yet another insurance claim denial, another flat tire, a home foreclosure or a terminal medical diagnosis.

After a while, the events of suffering merge and we are left with a vague feeling that the universe is mean-spirited.

Question: "Hey, what's going on?"

Answer: "Same shit, different day." (Thought bubble: I got stuck in a meeting today and was late picking up my son from daycare. Now I owe them an extra fifty bucks.)

Question: "How about you?"

Answer: "Same." (Thought bubble: My mother called me three times today wondering where her medications were. She'd already taken them. Then she forgot my name.)

Suffering manifests and dissolves. It takes ten thousand different forms. If we are lucky, we will be able to identify patterns here and there that allow us to eliminate some of the spinning wheels of samsara.

It still doesn't change the fundamental Noble Truth that life is suffering. Some would say it's perverse to refer to the events of the world as a repetition of bodily excrement, but I have to disagree. Like samsara, pooping is something we do every day. If we don't, it means there's something wrong. In a way, it's comforting to know there is one cycle we all share and in this whole impermanent world there is one thing we can count on: "Same shit, different day."

Learning to Stay

I am teaching my eight-year old daughter how to meditate. After a recent session in which she was squirming almost the entire time, I asked her how it went. She said: "I got distracted." Isn't that the perfect summary of months, if not years of our lives? "I got distracted." And why not? There's always something to think about.

It's humbling to observe the difficulty of being who we are, when we are, where we are, without reflexively constructing an imaginary universe that centers around us - one in which we are more exciting, perhaps, or more heroic. One in which we are sought out by others for advice and company. The current material culture surrounding us encourages us to value desirability and excitement over contentment and confuses the nature of happiness. There's always something to want.

When our ego is not being stroked into spending our last dime on a set of false eyelashes, our fight or flight mechanism is being triggered to panic. The future, being as yet untold contains every possible outcome of impermanence. Will our outcomes be what we had hoped, or will we be subject to ever deepening perhaps irreparable suffering? Will the bacteria on our kitchen sponge give us salmonella? Will we have enough to retire on comfortably, or will we spend our final years wrapped in layers of blankets to avoid paying for heating fuel? There is always something to worry about.

In terms of our ability to self-generate suffering, however, nothing beats obsessing on the past. Regret, guilt, shame, shoulda, coulda, woulda, if only I had...It is in our awareness of and attachment to the past that our losses aggregate. We remember those we loved who are gone. Hindsight allows us to appreciate opportunities we could have taken, but didn't. Time reveals options we didn't realize were available. There is always something to long for.

Looking ahead, looking behind, worry. The result is that we consistently live outside of the present moment. In *The Power of Now*, Ekart Tolle suggests a practical exercise to develop mindfulness for the present. When feeling upset, he instructs us to become aware of our surroundings and current condition and ask what is wrong with this moment right now. He proposes that we will usually discover the current moment is fine and that our mood is actually inspired by what we worry will happen in the future or what we wish we could change about the past. When I have tried this, I have found it often works.

There are many people who are smarter and more practiced than I am who have dedicated their lives to helping others find and enjoy the present moment. On occasion, I have tried a variety of strategies, but still I struggle with learning to "stay". Perhaps the father of the infamous Roseanne Roseannadanna expressed it the best: "It just goes to show you. It's always something. If it ain't one thing, it's another." Will I ever experience more than two consecutive moments of being entirely present in the now? Just thinking about it gets me distracted...

Katz!

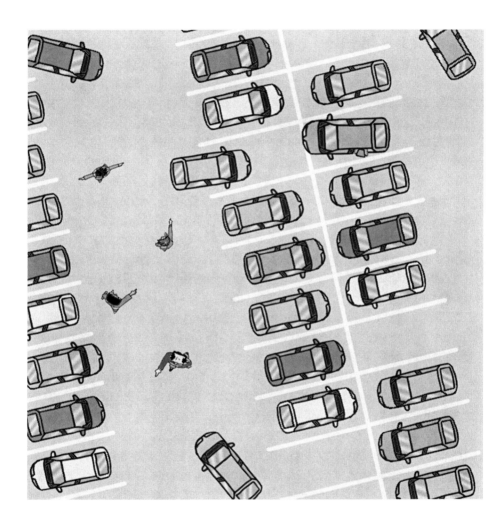

Do you remember reading Shakespeare in high school? Dry, dry, dry. Remember those awful, ancient productions featuring stiff actors with marbles in their mouths, who sawed their arms through space as they iambic pentametered the audience into a coma? Growing up, this was my only experience of Shakespeare. I was taught some "culture", but what good did it do me?

In 1995, I spent a month in Lenox, Massachusetts at Shakespeare & Company taking an intensive acting course. That's when I learned what Shakespeare was really all about. To give you some idea, the most popular t-shirt in the gift shop has the phrase "support debauchery, treachery and blackmail" written on the back. If Shakespeare were alive today, he'd be writing Matthew McConaughey movies, reality TV shows and soap operas.

I told you that to tell you this: It's important not to take all of this too seriously. The point of Buddhist practice is to find our way to a state of being where there is an absence of suffering - or at least a lessening of it. The fact that the physical and psychological conditions into which we have been born is stacked against us in this regard means very few of us will actually experience liberation in this lifetime.

For most of us, there is nothing but the journey toward nirvana. What sense would it make if the journey itself only intensifies the suffering we are trying to dissolve? If we can't laugh at our tendency to engage in the same unproductive thought patterns and behaviors repeatedly, what should we do? Perhaps we should saw our hands through the air shouting "To be or not to be? That is the question." It's really not a question though, is it? We be. Regardless of what conclusions we come to about the nature of that being and how to navigate impermanence and shenpa, we be. Katz!

Activities for Thought and Exploration

Often, I challenge myself to try experimental activities to illuminate or challenge some part of my practice as a Buddhist. The purpose of these, is to consider the dharma lessons that are hidden in all aspects of my daily life and develop a more consistent level of awareness of these lessons. Collected below, are some favorites I have tried. There is no particular order to the activity suggestions. Try whatever combination of activities that inspire you. Feel free to stop by the Average Buddhist blog, Facebook community or Google+ stream to share your experiences!

Mundane Mindfulness
Try performing mindfulness practice while completing "mundane" activities in your house. If you choose to fold the laundry, observe the texture of the fabric. Are the items warm or cool? Do any of the items trigger shenpa in one way or another? Consider trying this activity while washing the dishes, vacuuming, cleaning the toilet, helping your child with their homework, or anything else you want to explore.

Tolerance of Discomfort
Put yourself in a mildly uncomfortable situation. For example, go out on a chilly day without enough layers, walk around the block in the rain without an umbrella, fix yourself a meal made of things you don't like. While engaging in the activity make observations about your reactions. Do you have physical and/or emotional reactions? Do you label the situation or your reactions as "good" or "bad"? Does being in the uncomfortable situation bring up specific memories or fears? Once you get uncomfortable, are you tempted to terminate the activity immediately?

Tolerance of Discomfort - with Compassion Practice
Try the "Tolerance of Discomfort" activity again while doing Tonglen practice. Breathe in the suffering of people who experience these discomforts and do not have a choice. Breathe out healing and compassion.

Watcher of the Pack
Observe a pack of teenagers in your area - perhaps your own child and his/her friends. Think about the similarities and differences in the way they are dressed, how they are posturing themselves and who is talking to whom. What manifestations of craving can you see in their presentation and their mannerisms? Can you use these observations to illuminate some the hooks for things that trigger your craving? Is the manner of craving for you different or the same as when you were an adolescent? (Kids, try this one ten years from now)

Road Rage-less
While driving, try counting the number of times that you experience shenpa. When you catch yourself, explore the trigger. Are you making uncompassionate attributions to the behavior of other drivers? Are you accusing inanimate objects of having it out for you? Are you actually the one encountering resistance because you're the one disrupting the flow of traffic around you? Are you selfishly trying to get where you're going without considering others' concerns and circumstances? Be honest with yourself! If you repeat the activity numerous times, does the shenpa decrease?

Antici-patience,   You're   Makin'   You   Wait
Prepare or buy a favorite treat food (I tried this with a wrapped Kit Kat). Place it near you, but don't eat it right

away. Leave it there for a while intermittently taking a deep inhale of the scent. Do you feel craving or satisfaction? Frustration or anticipation? If the scent were all that were available to you, could you be satisfied with the scent alone?

Lifting the Curse
The next time you curse in frustration at a mundane inconvenience (e.g., dropping a stack of papers, stubbing your toe), pause and ask yourself if the cursing and the frustration were helpful in the current situation. Was there a conscious force that "made" this happen to you? Was there an army of inanimate objects conspiring against you? In that context, what was the purpose of cursing? Did it ease your suffering or amplify it?

Assumption Junction, What's Your Function
The next time someone is mean to you or inconveniences you in some way, notice your assumptions about why they did what they did. Did you automatically fill in the blanks with a negative assumption? If so, can you think of any alternative reasons or circumstances why they might have behaved the way they did? Was their behavior even necessarily related to the current moment, or might they be dealing with residual negativity from another area of their life?

Eye Need A Witness
Think of a past event you shared with another person. Get together with that person. Without consulting each other, each write down everything you remember about the event - the sequence of what happened, the sights, sounds and smells along with any other details. Compare

your versions of events. How similar are they? Where there are differences, how can you tell what "really" happened?

Nib-less
The next time you go to your favorite restaurant, order your favorite meal. When it arrives, divide each item in half and eat only half of each item in the dish. Allow the rest to stay on the plate, without picking at it while you converse with your companion. Does this cause stress? Is it difficult to prevent yourself from continuing to nibble after eating the apportioned amount? Feel free to take the rest home as leftovers, but don't eat any until the next day.

Wasting Away
The next time you are about to make an impulse buy of something you don't need, ask yourself what will happen to it when you don't want it any more. Will you keep it throughout its useful life? When you're done with it, can you recycle it? Can you donate it? Would someone want to purchase it on EBay? How long do you think it will be before you have to deal with the hassle of disposing of it in an ecologically sound manner? After going through this exercise, do you still want to buy it?

Treat You Right
The next time you are about to engage in a comfort activity that is harmful to you - with the excuse of "treating" yourself, ask yourself: "Is it really a treat if it's going to hurt me?" Consider the dual meaning of the word "treat" in that something can be a treat and one can also treat oneself in a particular way. Make a list of treats that are not self-destructive. Replace your self-destructive "treats" and keep your list with you for reference when you need it.

Task Master
Choose one hour of a workday to uni-task. Do not allow any interruptions. Don't check or respond to email, let phone calls go to voice mail, ask colleagues to return later if they need to speak with you (if you have an office door, close it). During this period of time, work on only one task. Is there a difference in the quality of the experience or in the work that is produced during the uni-tasking time period? What happens if you schedule in one uni-tasking hour per week? Per day?

Lessons In Lessons
Begin lessons in an activity you have never tried before. Observe your experience of being a student without mastery. Are you able to engage in the experience without frustration? Are you able to submit to being a student and not the one in charge? Can you accept the notion that you may never be a master at this activity and still enjoy the process? Ideas: singing, playing an instrument, sewing, knitting, woodworking, martial arts, dance.

Change of Pace – Slowing
If you have an elderly person in your life, try taking that person out for the day - perhaps to lunch or out shopping. Pace yourself to their pace and be careful not to rush them. What does it feel like to be moving at a different speed than is usual for you? Allow them to choose the topics of conversation. Are you able to enjoy the experience without feeling antsy?

Change of Pace – Bounding
If you have access to a young child, take them to a park and join them on the playground equipment. Allow them

to set the activity agenda. What does it feel like to move from activity to activity unpredictably? Can you keep up with the child's speed and modify the activities to accommodate your adult size? Are you able to enjoy the experience without worrying about what other adults might be thinking of you?

Liberalize Your Personal Conservatism
We all cling to certain notions of the way life "should" be and yet, there are quite diverging views on those should's. Choose a hot-button issue of yours and seek out opposing viewpoints on that issue. (Ideas: news broadcasts, newspapers, magazines, blogs, comments on blog posts) When digesting the opposing viewpoints, observe your reactions. How long does it take for the shenpa to begin? Do you find yourself making uncompassionate attributions about those who are expressing ideas that are different from your own? Are you able to consider alternatives to your negative attributions? Are you able to detrigger your shenpa without disengaging from the task?

Please Hold
Choose a period of time, two to three weeks, during which you will make only essential purchases. If there is anything you want to buy, but don't need as an essential at that moment, leave it until after the activity period. If you go food shopping, only buy what you will eat in that time period, nothing extra and no nonessential snacks or other items. Put all clothing, toy and gift purchases on hold. After the activity period is over, consider those things that you put a hold on buying and decide whether or not you still want to purchase them.

Photographic Memory
The next time you get something shiny and new (something that you'll be keeping for a while) take a picture of it. Use the thing as intended. One year later, take another picture of the item. (Don't forget to set a reminder for yourself in your personal calendar system) Notice how that thing is showing its wear. What pieces are breaking down? Is any part of it faded? Is it misshapen in any way? Are there scratches? If the object shows no sign of wear, what does that tell you? Was it something you didn't really need? Did you avoid using it as intended because you didn't want to "ruin" it? This is a great activity to do with cars, computers, sneakers, clothing or new power tools. For shorter durations, try nail polish a week after applying, make up at the end of a workday (no touch ups allowed), or coffee that's been allowed to sit on a desk for a week.

And You Are...?
What do you say when someone asks you about yourself? Do you tell them your profession, your role in the family, your religion, your political affiliation? Think about the first thing you usually reveal about yourself to someone new. Now imagine that thing is no longer true - blinked out, gone - not replaced by something else simply not there. What would you say instead? How does the way you introduce yourself impact your perception of yourself? Do you feel awkward having to reveal something different about yourself?

Count Me Out
Sit down in front of the TV some evening and watch prime time television. Keep a tally on a piece of paper of the jokes you hear. Categorize them according to whether or

not the joke is mean-spirited. Compare the tallies at the end of the evening and see what portion of the jokes were mean-spirited. How did you respond to the mean-spirited jokes? Would you have recognized them as mean-spirited, if you had not been involved in this activity? Try this same activity while observing bumper stickers, buttons or t-shirt slogans. How can one who lives for the development of compassion and the enlightenment of all sentient beings participate in humor and fun without betraying their commitment?

About the Author

By profession, Barbara is a voice-specialized speech-language pathologist and singing teacher. She has been an Average American Buddhist since 1994, having been introduced to the principles of the faith in Sogyul Rinpoche's *Tibetan Book of Living and Dying*. She furthered her practice in the Kwan Um School of Zen at the Cambridge Zen Center, but like many found it difficult to maintain regular contact with a Buddhist sangha after moving farther away from the city. This prompted her to reach out in creative ways to connect with like-minded dharma seekers around the country. She lives in Massachusetts with her husband, Teja, their two daughters and two cats.

About the Illustrator

Teja is a television producer, keynote speaker, college professor and illustrator. As a mixed-culture, race and ethnic American, and having grown up in Japan, he had spent years looking for meaning in identity. Although Buddhism has always been in the lexicon of everyday life for him, he did not formally embrace Buddhist philosophy until his late 30's. Teja identifies mostly with the cone on the Buddhi's head.

Be an Average Buddhist!
The Blog: http://www.averagebuddhist.com

On Facebook:
http://www.facebook.com/averagebuddhist

Average Buddhist is also active on Google+.

You can follow Average Buddhist on Twitter:
@averagebuddhist

CPSIA information can be obtained at www.ICGtesting.com
Printed in the USA
BVOW010510050412

286903BV00007B/28/P

9 781621 412212